50 Premium Wedding Cakes for Marriage

By: Kelly Johnson

Table of Contents

- Classic White Chocolate Raspberry Wedding Cake
- Lemon Elderflower Wedding Cake
- Red Velvet with Cream Cheese Frosting Wedding Cake
- Vanilla Bean and Champagne Wedding Cake
- Rich Chocolate Ganache Wedding Cake
- Almond and Pistachio Wedding Cake
- Lavender Honey Wedding Cake
- Strawberry and Champagne Wedding Cake
- Rose Water and Raspberry Wedding Cake
- Coconut and Lime Wedding Cake
- Carrot Cake with Cream Cheese Frosting
- Hazelnut and Chocolate Wedding Cake
- Fruitcake with Marzipan and Fondant
- Espresso and Mocha Wedding Cake
- Classic Marble Wedding Cake
- Lemon Blueberry Wedding Cake
- Peach and Vanilla Wedding Cake
- Salted Caramel and Chocolate Wedding Cake
- Caramelized Banana Wedding Cake
- Almond Raspberry Wedding Cake
- Mocha Hazelnut Wedding Cake
- Spiced Chai Latte Wedding Cake
- White Chocolate and Lemon Wedding Cake
- Strawberry Shortcake Wedding Cake
- Lemon and Rosemary Wedding Cake
- Honey and Pear Wedding Cake
- Gingerbread Spice Wedding Cake
- Blueberry and Vanilla Wedding Cake
- Pomegranate and White Chocolate Wedding Cake
- Mint Chocolate Chip Wedding Cake
- Mango and Coconut Wedding Cake
- Champagne and Peach Wedding Cake
- Coconut Cream Wedding Cake
- Black Forest Wedding Cake
- Raspberry and Vanilla Wedding Cake

- Poppy Seed Lemon Wedding Cake
- Apricot Almond Wedding Cake
- Tropical Fruit Wedding Cake
- Chocolate and Bourbon Wedding Cake
- Wildflower Honey Wedding Cake
- Red Wine and Chocolate Wedding Cake
- Marzipan and Dark Chocolate Wedding Cake
- Apple Cinnamon Wedding Cake
- Almond and Cherry Wedding Cake
- Citrus and Coconut Wedding Cake
- Raspberry Rose Wedding Cake
- Blackberry and Vanilla Wedding Cake
- Vanilla Bean with Passion Fruit Wedding Cake
- Mocha and Hazelnut Wedding Cake
- Lemon and Elderflower Sponge Wedding Cake

Classic White Chocolate Raspberry Wedding Cake

Ingredients:

- **For the cake:**
    - 2 1/2 cups all-purpose flour
    - 2 1/2 teaspoons baking powder
    - 1/2 teaspoon salt
    - 1 cup unsalted butter, softened
    - 1 1/2 cups sugar
    - 4 large eggs
    - 1 teaspoon vanilla extract
    - 1 cup whole milk
    - 1 cup white chocolate, melted
    - 1 cup fresh raspberries
- **For the frosting:**
    - 1 cup unsalted butter, softened
    - 4 cups powdered sugar
    - 1/2 cup white chocolate, melted
    - 2 teaspoons vanilla extract
    - 2-4 tablespoons heavy cream

Instructions:

1. **Prepare the Cake**
   Preheat the oven to 350°F (175°C). Grease and flour two 8-inch round cake pans. In a bowl, whisk together flour, baking powder, and salt. In another bowl, cream the butter and sugar until light and fluffy. Add the eggs one at a time, beating well after each addition. Mix in vanilla. Gradually add the flour mixture, alternating with milk. Fold in the melted white chocolate and raspberries.
2. **Bake the Cake**
   Divide the batter between the prepared pans. Bake for 30-35 minutes, or until a toothpick inserted comes out clean. Let the cakes cool in the pans for 10 minutes, then transfer to wire racks to cool completely.
3. **Prepare the Frosting**
   Beat the butter until smooth, then add powdered sugar in increments, beating until fluffy. Mix in melted white chocolate, vanilla, and enough heavy cream to achieve a smooth, spreadable consistency.

4. **Assemble the Cake**
   Frost the cooled cake layers with the white chocolate frosting. Decorate with additional fresh raspberries and white chocolate shavings if desired.

Lemon Elderflower Wedding Cake

Ingredients:

- **For the cake:**
    - 2 1/2 cups all-purpose flour
    - 2 1/2 teaspoons baking powder
    - 1/4 teaspoon salt
    - 1 cup unsalted butter, softened
    - 2 cups sugar
    - 4 large eggs
    - 1/4 cup lemon zest
    - 1/2 cup lemon juice
    - 1/2 cup elderflower cordial
    - 1 cup buttermilk
- **For the frosting:**
    - 1 cup unsalted butter, softened
    - 4 cups powdered sugar
    - 2 tablespoons elderflower cordial
    - 2 teaspoons lemon juice
    - 2-4 tablespoons heavy cream

Instructions:

1. **Prepare the Cake**
   Preheat the oven to 350°F (175°C). Grease and flour two 8-inch round cake pans. In a bowl, whisk together flour, baking powder, and salt. In another bowl, cream the butter and sugar until light and fluffy. Add the eggs one at a time, then mix in lemon zest, lemon juice, and elderflower cordial. Gradually add the flour mixture, alternating with buttermilk.
2. **Bake the Cake**
   Divide the batter between the prepared pans. Bake for 25-30 minutes, or until a toothpick inserted comes out clean. Let the cakes cool completely.
3. **Prepare the Frosting**
   Beat the butter until smooth, then add powdered sugar in increments, beating until fluffy. Mix in elderflower cordial, lemon juice, and enough heavy cream to reach a smooth, spreadable consistency.
4. **Assemble the Cake**
   Frost the cooled cakes with the elderflower frosting. Garnish with lemon slices and edible flowers for a decorative touch.

Red Velvet with Cream Cheese Frosting Wedding Cake

Ingredients:

- **For the cake:**
    - 2 1/2 cups all-purpose flour
    - 1 1/2 cups sugar
    - 1 teaspoon baking soda
    - 1 teaspoon salt
    - 1 tablespoon cocoa powder
    - 1 1/2 cups vegetable oil
    - 2 large eggs
    - 1 cup buttermilk
    - 2 tablespoons red food coloring
    - 1 teaspoon vanilla extract
    - 1 teaspoon white vinegar
- **For the frosting:**
    - 2 cups cream cheese, softened
    - 1/2 cup unsalted butter, softened
    - 4 cups powdered sugar
    - 2 teaspoons vanilla extract

Instructions:

1. **Prepare the Cake**
   Preheat the oven to 350°F (175°C). Grease and flour two 8-inch round cake pans. In a bowl, whisk together flour, sugar, baking soda, salt, and cocoa powder. In another bowl, beat together oil, eggs, buttermilk, food coloring, vanilla, and vinegar. Gradually add the dry ingredients to the wet ingredients, mixing until smooth.
2. **Bake the Cake**
   Divide the batter evenly between the pans and bake for 25-30 minutes, or until a toothpick comes out clean. Let the cakes cool completely.
3. **Prepare the Frosting**
   Beat the cream cheese and butter together until smooth. Gradually add powdered sugar and vanilla extract, mixing until fluffy.
4. **Assemble the Cake**
   Frost the cooled cakes with the cream cheese frosting. Decorate with red velvet cake crumbs or edible flowers.

Vanilla Bean and Champagne Wedding Cake

Ingredients:

- **For the cake:**
    - 2 1/2 cups all-purpose flour
    - 2 1/2 teaspoons baking powder
    - 1/4 teaspoon salt
    - 1 cup unsalted butter, softened
    - 2 cups sugar
    - 4 large eggs
    - 1 vanilla bean (seeds scraped)
    - 1 cup champagne
    - 1/2 cup buttermilk
- **For the frosting:**
    - 1 cup unsalted butter, softened
    - 4 cups powdered sugar
    - 1/2 cup champagne
    - 2 teaspoons vanilla extract

Instructions:

1. **Prepare the Cake**
   Preheat the oven to 350°F (175°C). Grease and flour two 8-inch round cake pans. In a bowl, whisk together flour, baking powder, and salt. In another bowl, cream the butter and sugar until light and fluffy. Add the eggs one at a time, beating well after each addition. Mix in vanilla bean seeds, champagne, and buttermilk. Gradually add the dry ingredients and mix until smooth.
2. **Bake the Cake**
   Divide the batter between the pans and bake for 25-30 minutes, or until a toothpick inserted comes out clean. Let the cakes cool completely.
3. **Prepare the Frosting**
   Beat the butter until smooth, then gradually add powdered sugar, champagne, and vanilla extract. Mix until fluffy.
4. **Assemble the Cake**
   Frost the cooled cakes with champagne frosting. Decorate with champagne-flavored decorations or edible gold leaf.

Rich Chocolate Ganache Wedding Cake

Ingredients:

- **For the cake:**
    - 2 1/2 cups all-purpose flour
    - 1 1/2 teaspoons baking powder
    - 1/2 teaspoon baking soda
    - 1 teaspoon salt
    - 1 cup unsalted butter, softened
    - 1 1/2 cups sugar
    - 3 large eggs
    - 1 cup unsweetened cocoa powder
    - 1 cup whole milk
    - 1 teaspoon vanilla extract
    - 1 cup boiling water
- **For the ganache:**
    - 1 1/2 cups heavy cream
    - 1 1/2 cups semi-sweet chocolate chips
    - 1 tablespoon unsalted butter

Instructions:

1. **Prepare the Cake**
   Preheat the oven to 350°F (175°C). Grease and flour two 8-inch round cake pans. In a bowl, whisk together flour, baking powder, baking soda, salt, and cocoa powder. In another bowl, cream the butter and sugar until fluffy. Add eggs one at a time, mixing well after each addition. Gradually add the dry ingredients, alternating with milk. Stir in the vanilla extract, then mix in the boiling water.
2. **Bake the Cake**
   Divide the batter between the pans and bake for 30-35 minutes, or until a toothpick inserted comes out clean. Let the cakes cool completely.
3. **Prepare the Ganache**
   Heat the heavy cream in a saucepan over medium heat until it starts to simmer. Pour over the chocolate chips and stir until smooth. Add butter and mix until glossy.
4. **Assemble the Cake**
   Frost the cooled cakes with the ganache. Decorate with chocolate curls or berries.

Almond and Pistachio Wedding Cake

Ingredients:

- **For the cake:**
    - 2 1/2 cups all-purpose flour
    - 1 1/2 teaspoons baking powder
    - 1/4 teaspoon salt
    - 1 cup unsalted butter, softened
    - 1 1/2 cups sugar
    - 4 large eggs
    - 1 teaspoon almond extract
    - 1 cup whole milk
    - 1/2 cup finely ground pistachios
- **For the frosting:**
    - 1 cup unsalted butter, softened
    - 4 cups powdered sugar
    - 1/4 cup pistachio paste
    - 1 teaspoon almond extract
    - 2 tablespoons milk

Instructions:

1. **Prepare the Cake**
   Preheat the oven to 350°F (175°C). Grease and flour two 8-inch round cake pans. In a bowl, whisk together flour, baking powder, and salt. In another bowl, cream the butter and sugar until light and fluffy. Add eggs one at a time, mixing well after each addition. Stir in almond extract and ground pistachios. Gradually add the dry ingredients and milk.
2. **Bake the Cake**
   Divide the batter between the pans and bake for 30-35 minutes, or until a toothpick inserted comes out clean. Let the cakes cool completely.
3. **Prepare the Frosting**
   Beat the butter until smooth, then add powdered sugar, pistachio paste, almond extract, and milk. Mix until smooth.
4. **Assemble the Cake**
   Frost the cooled cakes with pistachio frosting. Garnish with chopped pistachios or toasted almonds.

Lavender Honey Wedding Cake

Ingredients:

- **For the cake:**
    - 2 1/2 cups all-purpose flour
    - 1 1/2 teaspoons baking powder
    - 1/2 teaspoon salt
    - 1 cup unsalted butter, softened
    - 2 cups sugar
    - 4 large eggs
    - 1 tablespoon lavender buds
    - 1/2 cup honey
    - 1/2 cup whole milk
- **For the frosting:**
    - 1 cup unsalted butter, softened
    - 4 cups powdered sugar
    - 2 tablespoons honey
    - 1 teaspoon vanilla extract
    - 2-4 tablespoons heavy cream

Instructions:

1. **Prepare the Cake**
   Preheat the oven to 350°F (175°C). Grease and flour two 8-inch round cake pans. In a bowl, whisk together flour, baking powder, and salt. In another bowl, cream the butter and sugar until light and fluffy. Add eggs one at a time, mixing well after each addition. Mix in lavender buds, honey, and milk.
2. **Bake the Cake**
   Divide the batter between the pans and bake for 25-30 minutes, or until a toothpick comes out clean. Let the cakes cool completely.
3. **Prepare the Frosting**
   Beat the butter until smooth, then add powdered sugar, honey, vanilla extract, and enough heavy cream to reach a smooth consistency.
4. **Assemble the Cake**
   Frost the cooled cakes with the honey frosting. Decorate with sprigs of lavender or edible flowers.

Strawberry and Champagne Wedding Cake

Ingredients:

- **For the cake:**
    - 2 1/2 cups all-purpose flour
    - 1 1/2 teaspoons baking powder
    - 1/4 teaspoon salt
    - 1 cup unsalted butter, softened
    - 2 cups sugar
    - 4 large eggs
    - 1/2 cup champagne
    - 1 teaspoon vanilla extract
    - 1 cup pureed strawberries
- **For the frosting:**
    - 1 cup unsalted butter, softened
    - 4 cups powdered sugar
    - 1/2 cup champagne
    - 2 teaspoons vanilla extract
    - 1/4 cup pureed strawberries

Instructions:

1. **Prepare the Cake**
   Preheat the oven to 350°F (175°C). Grease and flour two 8-inch round cake pans. In a bowl, whisk together flour, baking powder, and salt. In another bowl, cream the butter and sugar until light and fluffy. Add the eggs one at a time, then mix in champagne, vanilla extract, and strawberry puree.
2. **Bake the Cake**
   Divide the batter between the pans and bake for 25-30 minutes, or until a toothpick inserted comes out clean. Let the cakes cool completely.
3. **Prepare the Frosting**
   Beat the butter until smooth, then add powdered sugar, champagne, vanilla extract, and strawberry puree. Mix until fluffy.
4. **Assemble the Cake**
   Frost the cooled cakes with the strawberry champagne frosting. Decorate with fresh strawberries or champagne-flavored decorations.

Rose Water and Raspberry Wedding Cake

Ingredients:

- **For the cake:**
    - 2 1/2 cups all-purpose flour
    - 1 1/2 teaspoons baking powder
    - 1/4 teaspoon salt
    - 1 cup unsalted butter, softened
    - 2 cups sugar
    - 4 large eggs
    - 1 teaspoon rose water
    - 1 cup whole milk
    - 1/2 cup fresh raspberries
- **For the frosting:**
    - 1 cup unsalted butter, softened
    - 4 cups powdered sugar
    - 1 teaspoon rose water
    - 2-4 tablespoons heavy cream
    - Fresh raspberries for garnish

Instructions:

1. **Prepare the Cake**
   Preheat the oven to 350°F (175°C). Grease and flour two 8-inch round cake pans. In a bowl, whisk together flour, baking powder, and salt. In another bowl, cream the butter and sugar until light and fluffy. Add eggs one at a time, mixing well after each addition. Mix in rose water, milk, and raspberries.
2. **Bake the Cake**
   Divide the batter between the pans and bake for 25-30 minutes, or until a toothpick inserted comes out clean. Let the cakes cool completely.
3. **Prepare the Frosting**
   Beat the butter until smooth, then add powdered sugar, rose water, and enough heavy cream to reach a smooth, spreadable consistency.
4. **Assemble the Cake**
   Frost the cooled cakes with the rose water frosting. Garnish with fresh raspberries and edible flowers for a beautiful presentation.

Coconut and Lime Wedding Cake

Ingredients:

- **For the cake:**
    - 2 1/2 cups all-purpose flour
    - 1 1/2 teaspoons baking powder
    - 1/2 teaspoon salt
    - 1 cup unsalted butter, softened
    - 2 cups sugar
    - 4 large eggs
    - 1 cup shredded coconut
    - Zest of 2 limes
    - 1/2 cup fresh lime juice
    - 1/2 cup whole milk
- **For the frosting:**
    - 1 cup unsalted butter, softened
    - 4 cups powdered sugar
    - 2 tablespoons fresh lime juice
    - 1/2 cup shredded coconut for garnish

Instructions:

1. **Prepare the Cake**
   Preheat the oven to 350°F (175°C). Grease and flour two 8-inch round cake pans. In a bowl, whisk together flour, baking powder, and salt. In another bowl, cream the butter and sugar until light and fluffy. Add the eggs one at a time, mixing well after each addition. Stir in coconut, lime zest, lime juice, and milk.
2. **Bake the Cake**
   Divide the batter between the pans and bake for 25-30 minutes, or until a toothpick comes out clean. Let the cakes cool completely.
3. **Prepare the Frosting**
   Beat the butter until smooth, then add powdered sugar and lime juice. Mix until fluffy and smooth.
4. **Assemble the Cake**
   Frost the cooled cakes with the lime frosting and garnish with shredded coconut.

Carrot Cake with Cream Cheese Frosting

Ingredients:

- **For the cake:**
    - 2 1/2 cups all-purpose flour
    - 1 1/2 teaspoons baking powder
    - 1 teaspoon baking soda
    - 1 1/2 teaspoons ground cinnamon
    - 1/4 teaspoon ground nutmeg
    - 1/2 teaspoon salt
    - 1 1/2 cups vegetable oil
    - 2 cups sugar
    - 4 large eggs
    - 2 teaspoons vanilla extract
    - 3 cups grated carrots
    - 1/2 cup chopped walnuts (optional)
- **For the frosting:**
    - 1 cup cream cheese, softened
    - 1/2 cup unsalted butter, softened
    - 4 cups powdered sugar
    - 1 teaspoon vanilla extract

Instructions:

1. **Prepare the Cake**
   Preheat the oven to 350°F (175°C). Grease and flour two 8-inch round cake pans. In a bowl, whisk together flour, baking powder, baking soda, cinnamon, nutmeg, and salt. In another bowl, whisk together oil, sugar, eggs, and vanilla extract. Stir in grated carrots and optional walnuts. Gradually add dry ingredients and mix until combined.
2. **Bake the Cake**
   Divide the batter between the pans and bake for 30-35 minutes, or until a toothpick comes out clean. Let the cakes cool completely.
3. **Prepare the Frosting**
   Beat together the cream cheese and butter until smooth. Gradually add powdered sugar and vanilla extract, beating until fluffy.
4. **Assemble the Cake**
   Frost the cooled cakes with cream cheese frosting. Garnish with additional chopped walnuts if desired.

Hazelnut and Chocolate Wedding Cake

Ingredients:

- **For the cake:**
    - 2 1/2 cups all-purpose flour
    - 1 1/2 teaspoons baking powder
    - 1/2 teaspoon salt
    - 1 cup unsalted butter, softened
    - 1 1/2 cups sugar
    - 4 large eggs
    - 1 teaspoon vanilla extract
    - 1 cup hazelnut flour
    - 1 cup cocoa powder
    - 1/2 cup whole milk
- **For the frosting:**
    - 1 cup unsalted butter, softened
    - 3 cups powdered sugar
    - 1/2 cup cocoa powder
    - 1 teaspoon vanilla extract
    - 2 tablespoons heavy cream

Instructions:

1. **Prepare the Cake**
   Preheat the oven to 350°F (175°C). Grease and flour two 8-inch round cake pans. In a bowl, whisk together flour, baking powder, salt, hazelnut flour, and cocoa powder. In another bowl, cream the butter and sugar until light and fluffy. Add eggs one at a time, then stir in vanilla extract. Gradually add the dry ingredients, alternating with milk, and mix until smooth.
2. **Bake the Cake**
   Divide the batter between the pans and bake for 30-35 minutes, or until a toothpick comes out clean. Let the cakes cool completely.
3. **Prepare the Frosting**
   Beat the butter until smooth, then add powdered sugar, cocoa powder, vanilla extract, and heavy cream. Beat until smooth and fluffy.
4. **Assemble the Cake**
   Frost the cooled cakes with the chocolate hazelnut frosting. Decorate with chopped hazelnuts if desired.

Fruitcake with Marzipan and Fondant

Ingredients:

- **For the cake:**
    - 2 cups mixed dried fruit (raisins, currants, sultanas)
    - 1 cup mixed candied peel
    - 1 cup unsalted butter, softened
    - 1 1/2 cups brown sugar
    - 4 large eggs
    - 2 1/2 cups all-purpose flour
    - 1 teaspoon baking powder
    - 1 teaspoon ground cinnamon
    - 1 teaspoon ground nutmeg
    - 1/2 teaspoon salt
    - 1/4 cup brandy or orange juice
    - 1 cup chopped nuts (optional)
    - 1/4 cup molasses
- **For the frosting:**
    - 1 cup marzipan
    - 1/2 cup apricot jam (for glaze)
    - 1/2 cup fondant

Instructions:

1. **Prepare the Cake**
   Preheat the oven to 325°F (165°C). Grease and line an 8-inch round cake pan. In a bowl, mix dried fruit, candied peel, and nuts. In another bowl, cream butter and sugar until light and fluffy. Add eggs one at a time. In a separate bowl, whisk together flour, baking powder, cinnamon, nutmeg, and salt. Gradually add the dry ingredients and molasses. Stir in brandy or orange juice.
2. **Bake the Cake**
   Add the fruit mixture to the batter, then bake for 1 hour 30 minutes, or until a toothpick comes out clean. Let the cake cool.
3. **Prepare the Frosting**
   Warm apricot jam and spread it over the cooled cake as a glaze. Roll out marzipan and place it on top. Add fondant on top of the marzipan.
4. **Assemble the Cake**
   Decorate with fondant and marzipan. Allow it to set before serving.

Espresso and Mocha Wedding Cake

Ingredients:

- **For the cake:**
    - 2 1/2 cups all-purpose flour
    - 1 1/2 teaspoons baking powder
    - 1/2 teaspoon salt
    - 1 cup unsalted butter, softened
    - 2 cups sugar
    - 4 large eggs
    - 1/2 cup strong brewed espresso
    - 1 teaspoon vanilla extract
    - 1/2 cup cocoa powder
    - 1/2 cup whole milk
- **For the frosting:**
    - 1 cup unsalted butter, softened
    - 3 cups powdered sugar
    - 1/4 cup cocoa powder
    - 1 tablespoon espresso powder
    - 2 tablespoons heavy cream

Instructions:

1. **Prepare the Cake**
   Preheat the oven to 350°F (175°C). Grease and flour two 8-inch round cake pans. In a bowl, whisk together flour, baking powder, salt, cocoa powder. In another bowl, cream butter and sugar until light and fluffy. Add eggs one at a time, then mix in brewed espresso and vanilla extract. Gradually add the dry ingredients and milk.
2. **Bake the Cake**
   Divide the batter between the pans and bake for 30-35 minutes, or until a toothpick comes out clean. Let the cakes cool completely.
3. **Prepare the Frosting**
   Beat the butter until smooth, then add powdered sugar, cocoa powder, espresso powder, and heavy cream. Beat until smooth and fluffy.
4. **Assemble the Cake**
   Frost the cooled cakes with mocha frosting and decorate with chocolate shavings or espresso beans.

Classic Marble Wedding Cake

Ingredients:

- **For the cake:**
    - 2 1/2 cups all-purpose flour
    - 1 1/2 teaspoons baking powder
    - 1/4 teaspoon salt
    - 1 cup unsalted butter, softened
    - 2 cups sugar
    - 4 large eggs
    - 1 teaspoon vanilla extract
    - 1/2 cup whole milk
    - 1/2 cup cocoa powder
- **For the frosting:**
    - 1 cup unsalted butter, softened
    - 4 cups powdered sugar
    - 2 teaspoons vanilla extract
    - 1/4 cup whole milk

Instructions:

1. **Prepare the Cake**
   Preheat the oven to 350°F (175°C). Grease and flour two 8-inch round cake pans. In a bowl, whisk together flour, baking powder, and salt. In another bowl, cream the butter and sugar until light and fluffy. Add eggs one at a time, then stir in vanilla extract and milk. Divide the batter in half. Add cocoa powder to one half and stir to combine.
2. **Bake the Cake**
   Alternate spooning the vanilla and chocolate batters into the pans. Swirl gently with a knife for a marble effect. Bake for 30-35 minutes, or until a toothpick comes out clean. Let the cakes cool completely.
3. **Prepare the Frosting**
   Beat the butter until smooth, then add powdered sugar, vanilla extract, and enough milk to reach a smooth consistency.
4. **Assemble the Cake**
   Frost the cooled cakes with vanilla frosting. Decorate with chocolate shavings or a marble effect.

Lemon Blueberry Wedding Cake

Ingredients:

- **For the cake:**
    - 2 1/2 cups all-purpose flour
    - 1 1/2 teaspoons baking powder
    - 1/4 teaspoon salt
    - 1 cup unsalted butter, softened
    - 2 cups sugar
    - 4 large eggs
    - Zest of 2 lemons
    - 1/2 cup whole milk
    - 1 cup fresh blueberries
- **For the frosting:**
    - 1 cup unsalted butter, softened
    - 4 cups powdered sugar
    - 2 tablespoons lemon juice
    - Zest of 1 lemon

Instructions:

1. **Prepare the Cake**
   Preheat the oven to 350°F (175°C). Grease and flour two 8-inch round cake pans. In a bowl, whisk together flour, baking powder, and salt. In another bowl, cream the butter and sugar until light and fluffy. Add eggs one at a time, then stir in lemon zest and milk. Fold in blueberries.
2. **Bake the Cake**
   Divide the batter between the pans and bake for 25-30 minutes, or until a toothpick comes out clean. Let the cakes cool completely.
3. **Prepare the Frosting**
   Beat the butter until smooth, then add powdered sugar, lemon juice, and lemon zest. Beat until smooth and fluffy.
4. **Assemble the Cake**
   Frost the cooled cakes with lemon frosting. Garnish with fresh blueberries or lemon slices.

Peach and Vanilla Wedding Cake

Ingredients:

- **For the cake:**
    - 2 1/2 cups all-purpose flour
    - 1 1/2 teaspoons baking powder
    - 1/4 teaspoon salt
    - 1 cup unsalted butter, softened
    - 2 cups sugar
    - 4 large eggs
    - 1 teaspoon vanilla extract
    - 1/2 cup whole milk
    - 1 cup fresh peach puree
- **For the frosting:**
    - 1 cup unsalted butter, softened
    - 4 cups powdered sugar
    - 2 teaspoons vanilla extract
    - 2 tablespoons heavy cream

Instructions:

1. **Prepare the Cake**
   Preheat the oven to 350°F (175°C). Grease and flour two 8-inch round cake pans. In a bowl, whisk together flour, baking powder, and salt. In another bowl, cream the butter and sugar until light and fluffy. Add eggs one at a time, then stir in vanilla extract and milk. Fold in peach puree.
2. **Bake the Cake**
   Divide the batter between the pans and bake for 25-30 minutes, or until a toothpick comes out clean. Let the cakes cool completely.
3. **Prepare the Frosting**
   Beat the butter until smooth, then add powdered sugar, vanilla extract, and heavy cream. Beat until smooth and fluffy.
4. **Assemble the Cake**
   Frost the cooled cakes with peach vanilla frosting. Garnish with fresh peach slices or flowers.

Salted Caramel and Chocolate Wedding Cake

Ingredients:

For the Chocolate Cake:

- 2 1/2 cups all-purpose flour
- 2 1/2 tsp baking powder
- 1 tsp baking soda
- 1/2 tsp salt
- 1 cup unsweetened cocoa powder
- 1 1/2 cups granulated sugar
- 1 cup whole milk
- 1/2 cup vegetable oil
- 2 large eggs
- 1 tsp vanilla extract
- 1 cup hot water (or strong brewed coffee for a deeper flavor)

For the Salted Caramel:

- 1 cup granulated sugar
- 6 tbsp unsalted butter, cut into pieces
- 1/2 cup heavy cream
- 1 tsp vanilla extract
- 1/2 tsp sea salt

For the Chocolate Ganache:

- 8 oz dark chocolate (60% cocoa)
- 1/2 cup heavy cream
- 2 tbsp unsalted butter

For the Frosting:

- 1 cup unsalted butter, softened
- 1/2 cup salted caramel sauce (from the recipe above)
- 4 cups powdered sugar, sifted
- 2 tbsp milk
- Pinch of salt (if needed)

Instructions:

1. Make the Chocolate Cake:

- Preheat your oven to 350°F (175°C). Grease and flour three 8-inch round cake pans.
- In a large bowl, whisk together the flour, baking powder, baking soda, salt, cocoa powder, and sugar.
- Add the milk, oil, eggs, and vanilla extract. Mix until smooth.
- Gradually add the hot water (or coffee), mixing until the batter is thin but well combined.
- Pour the batter evenly into the prepared pans. Bake for 30-35 minutes, or until a toothpick inserted comes out clean.
- Let the cakes cool in the pans for 10 minutes, then transfer to wire racks to cool completely.

2. Make the Salted Caramel:

- In a medium saucepan over medium heat, melt the sugar until it turns amber in color, swirling the pan occasionally.
- Once the sugar has melted, carefully add the butter and stir until combined.
- Gradually add the heavy cream, stirring constantly until smooth. Let it boil for 1-2 minutes, then remove from heat.
- Stir in the vanilla extract and sea salt. Set aside to cool.

3. Make the Chocolate Ganache:

- Place the dark chocolate in a heatproof bowl. In a small saucepan, bring the heavy cream to a simmer over medium heat.
- Pour the hot cream over the chocolate and let it sit for 2-3 minutes. Stir until smooth and glossy.
- Stir in the butter until fully combined. Set aside to cool and thicken.

4. Make the Frosting:

- Beat the softened butter in a large bowl until creamy and smooth.
- Gradually add the sifted powdered sugar, mixing well after each addition.
- Add the salted caramel sauce and mix until combined. If the frosting is too thick, add a tablespoon of milk at a time until it reaches a spreadable consistency.
- Taste and add a pinch of salt if desired.

5. Assemble the Cake:

- Place the first layer of chocolate cake on a cake board or serving platter. Spread a layer of salted caramel frosting on top.
- Drizzle some salted caramel sauce over the frosting.
- Add the second layer of cake and repeat the frosting and caramel steps.
- Top with the final cake layer and frost the entire cake with the salted caramel buttercream frosting.
- Decorate the sides and top with chocolate ganache, either by drizzling it or spreading it evenly. You can also pipe extra frosting for a decorative finish.

6. Serve and Enjoy:

- Once the cake is assembled, refrigerate for at least 30 minutes to allow the ganache to set.
- Slice and enjoy your decadent, wedding-worthy salted caramel and chocolate cake!

Salted Caramel and Chocolate Wedding Cake

Ingredients:

For the Chocolate Cake:

- 2 1/2 cups all-purpose flour
- 1 1/2 cups unsweetened cocoa powder
- 1 1/2 teaspoons baking powder
- 1 1/2 teaspoons baking soda
- 1 teaspoon salt
- 2 cups granulated sugar
- 1 cup unsalted butter, softened
- 4 large eggs
- 1 teaspoon vanilla extract
- 1 cup whole milk
- 1 cup hot water
- 1 cup sour cream

For the Salted Caramel Filling:

- 1 1/2 cups granulated sugar
- 6 tablespoons unsalted butter
- 1/2 cup heavy cream
- 1 teaspoon vanilla extract
- 1/2 teaspoon sea salt

For the Chocolate Ganache:

- 8 oz semi-sweet chocolate, chopped
- 1 cup heavy cream
- 2 tablespoons unsalted butter
- 1 teaspoon vanilla extract

For the Buttercream Frosting:

- 1 cup unsalted butter, softened
- 4 cups powdered sugar
- 1/4 cup heavy cream
- 1 teaspoon vanilla extract
- Pinch of salt

Instructions:

For the Chocolate Cake:

1. Preheat your oven to 350°F (175°C). Grease and flour three 8-inch cake pans.
2. In a medium bowl, whisk together flour, cocoa powder, baking powder, baking soda, and salt.
3. In a large bowl, beat the sugar and butter together until light and fluffy, about 3-5 minutes.
4. Add the eggs one at a time, beating well after each addition. Stir in the vanilla extract.
5. Gradually add the dry ingredients to the wet ingredients, alternating with the milk, beginning and ending with the dry ingredients. Mix until just combined.
6. Add the sour cream and stir until smooth.
7. Divide the batter evenly among the cake pans.
8. Bake for 30-35 minutes, or until a toothpick inserted in the center comes out clean.
9. Let the cakes cool in the pans for 10 minutes, then remove them from the pans and cool completely on a wire rack.

For the Salted Caramel Filling:

1. In a medium saucepan over medium heat, melt the sugar, stirring constantly until it turns amber (about 5-7 minutes).
2. Carefully add the butter, whisking until melted and smooth.
3. Slowly pour in the heavy cream while continuing to whisk until fully incorporated.
4. Remove from heat and stir in the vanilla extract and sea salt.
5. Let the caramel cool to room temperature before using.

For the Chocolate Ganache:

1. Place the chopped chocolate in a heatproof bowl.
2. Heat the heavy cream in a saucepan over medium heat until it begins to simmer.
3. Pour the cream over the chocolate and let it sit for 2-3 minutes. Then, whisk until smooth and glossy.
4. Stir in the butter and vanilla extract. Allow it to cool to room temperature before using.

For the Buttercream Frosting:

1. Beat the softened butter on medium speed until smooth and creamy, about 3 minutes.
2. Gradually add the powdered sugar, 1 cup at a time, and beat until fluffy.
3. Add the heavy cream, vanilla extract, and a pinch of salt, and beat until light and smooth.

Assembling the Cake:

1. Place one layer of chocolate cake on a serving plate. Spread a layer of salted caramel filling on top.
2. Add the second layer of cake and repeat the caramel layer.
3. Place the third layer of cake on top and frost the entire cake with buttercream frosting.
4. Drizzle the cooled chocolate ganache over the top of the cake, allowing it to drip down the sides.
5. Finish by sprinkling a pinch of sea salt over the top for an extra touch of flavor.

Caramelized Banana Wedding Cake

Ingredients:

For the Banana Cake:

- 2 1/2 cups all-purpose flour
- 2 teaspoons baking powder
- 1/2 teaspoon baking soda
- 1/2 teaspoon salt
- 1 cup unsalted butter, softened
- 1 1/2 cups granulated sugar
- 4 large eggs
- 1 teaspoon vanilla extract
- 1 1/2 cups mashed ripe bananas (about 4 bananas)
- 1 cup sour cream

For the Caramelized Bananas:

- 4 ripe bananas, sliced
- 1/2 cup brown sugar
- 2 tablespoons unsalted butter
- 1/2 teaspoon vanilla extract

For the Buttercream Frosting:

- 1 cup unsalted butter, softened
- 4 cups powdered sugar
- 1/4 cup heavy cream
- 1 teaspoon vanilla extract
- Pinch of salt

Instructions:

1. **For the Banana Cake:**
    - Preheat your oven to 350°F (175°C). Grease and flour three 8-inch round cake pans.
    - In a medium bowl, whisk together the flour, baking powder, baking soda, and salt.
    - In a large bowl, beat the butter and sugar together until light and fluffy, about 3-5 minutes.

- Add the eggs one at a time, mixing well after each addition. Stir in the vanilla extract.
- Gradually add the flour mixture to the wet ingredients, alternating with the mashed bananas and sour cream. Start and finish with the dry ingredients.
- Divide the batter evenly among the prepared cake pans.
- Bake for 25-30 minutes, or until a toothpick inserted into the center comes out clean.
- Cool the cakes in the pans for 10 minutes, then transfer to a wire rack to cool completely.

2. **For the Caramelized Bananas:**
   - In a skillet over medium heat, melt the butter and brown sugar.
   - Add the banana slices and cook for 3-4 minutes, stirring occasionally, until the bananas are soft and caramelized.
   - Remove from heat and stir in the vanilla extract. Let cool.

3. **For the Buttercream Frosting:**
   - Beat the softened butter on medium speed until smooth and creamy.
   - Gradually add the powdered sugar, 1 cup at a time, and continue beating until fluffy.
   - Add the heavy cream, vanilla extract, and a pinch of salt, and mix until smooth.

4. **Assembling the Cake:**
   - Place one layer of banana cake on a serving plate.
   - Spread a layer of buttercream frosting on top, followed by a layer of caramelized bananas.
   - Repeat with the next layer of cake, frosting, and caramelized bananas.
   - Frost the entire cake with the remaining buttercream frosting and decorate with additional caramelized bananas on top.

Almond Raspberry Wedding Cake

Ingredients:

For the Almond Cake:

- 2 1/2 cups all-purpose flour
- 1 teaspoon baking powder
- 1/2 teaspoon salt
- 1 cup unsalted butter, softened
- 1 1/4 cups granulated sugar
- 4 large eggs
- 1 teaspoon almond extract
- 1/2 teaspoon vanilla extract
- 1 cup whole milk
- 1/2 cup finely ground almonds (almond meal)

For the Raspberry Filling:

- 2 cups fresh raspberries
- 1/2 cup granulated sugar
- 1 tablespoon lemon juice
- 1 tablespoon cornstarch mixed with 1 tablespoon water (optional, for thickening)

For the Almond Buttercream Frosting:

- 1 cup unsalted butter, softened
- 4 cups powdered sugar
- 1/4 cup heavy cream
- 1 teaspoon almond extract
- Pinch of salt

Instructions:

1. **For the Almond Cake:**
   - Preheat your oven to 350°F (175°C). Grease and flour three 8-inch round cake pans.
   - In a medium bowl, whisk together the flour, baking powder, and salt.
   - In a large bowl, beat the butter and sugar together until light and fluffy.
   - Add the eggs one at a time, mixing well after each addition. Stir in the almond and vanilla extracts.

- Gradually add the dry ingredients to the wet ingredients, alternating with the milk, and mix until smooth.
- Stir in the almond meal.
- Divide the batter evenly between the prepared pans.
- Bake for 25-30 minutes, or until a toothpick inserted in the center comes out clean.
- Cool the cakes in the pans for 10 minutes, then remove them from the pans and cool completely on a wire rack.

2. **For the Raspberry Filling:**
    - In a saucepan over medium heat, combine the raspberries, sugar, and lemon juice. Cook for about 10 minutes, until the raspberries break down and the mixture thickens.
    - If you want a thicker filling, mix the cornstarch with water and add to the raspberry mixture. Cook for an additional 2-3 minutes, stirring constantly.
    - Remove from heat and allow to cool.

3. **For the Almond Buttercream Frosting:**
    - Beat the butter on medium speed until smooth and creamy.
    - Gradually add the powdered sugar, 1 cup at a time, and continue beating until fluffy.
    - Add the heavy cream, almond extract, and salt, and mix until smooth.

4. **Assembling the Cake:**
    - Place one layer of almond cake on a serving plate.
    - Spread a layer of raspberry filling over the cake, followed by a layer of almond buttercream.
    - Add the second layer of cake, repeat with raspberry filling and frosting.
    - Top with the final layer of cake and cover the entire cake with almond buttercream.
    - Decorate with fresh raspberries and slivers of toasted almonds.

Mocha Hazelnut Wedding Cake

Ingredients:

For the Mocha Cake:

- 2 1/2 cups all-purpose flour
- 1 1/2 teaspoons baking powder
- 1 teaspoon baking soda
- 1/2 teaspoon salt
- 1 cup unsalted butter, softened
- 1 1/2 cups granulated sugar
- 4 large eggs
- 1 teaspoon vanilla extract
- 1/2 cup brewed espresso, cooled
- 1 cup sour cream
- 1/2 cup chopped hazelnuts

For the Mocha Buttercream Frosting:

- 1 cup unsalted butter, softened
- 4 cups powdered sugar
- 1/4 cup heavy cream
- 1/4 cup brewed espresso, cooled
- 1/2 teaspoon vanilla extract
- Pinch of salt

For the Hazelnut Praline:

- 1 cup hazelnuts, toasted and chopped
- 1/2 cup granulated sugar
- 1/4 cup water

Instructions:

1. **For the Mocha Cake:**
    - Preheat your oven to 350°F (175°C). Grease and flour three 8-inch cake pans.
    - In a medium bowl, whisk together the flour, baking powder, baking soda, and salt.

- In a large bowl, beat the butter and sugar until light and fluffy. Add the eggs one at a time, mixing well after each addition. Stir in the vanilla extract.
- Gradually add the dry ingredients to the wet ingredients, alternating with the espresso and sour cream. Mix until smooth.
- Fold in the chopped hazelnuts.
- Divide the batter evenly between the cake pans and bake for 30-35 minutes, or until a toothpick inserted in the center comes out clean. Cool the cakes in the pans for 10 minutes, then transfer to a wire rack to cool completely.

2. **For the Mocha Buttercream:**
    - Beat the butter on medium speed until smooth and creamy.
    - Gradually add the powdered sugar, one cup at a time, and continue beating until fluffy.
    - Add the heavy cream, espresso, vanilla extract, and salt. Mix until smooth.

3. **For the Hazelnut Praline:**
    - In a saucepan, melt the sugar with the water over medium heat, swirling the pan occasionally until it turns amber.
    - Stir in the toasted hazelnuts and cook for another 2-3 minutes.
    - Pour the praline onto a parchment-lined baking sheet and let it cool. Once hardened, break into pieces.

4. **Assembling the Cake:**
    - Place one layer of mocha cake on a serving plate and spread with mocha buttercream.
    - Repeat with the second layer of cake and frosting.
    - Frost the entire cake and garnish with the hazelnut praline pieces on top.

Spiced Chai Latte Wedding Cake

Ingredients:

For the Chai Cake:

- 2 1/2 cups all-purpose flour
- 1 teaspoon baking powder
- 1 teaspoon baking soda
- 1/2 teaspoon ground cinnamon
- 1/2 teaspoon ground ginger
- 1/4 teaspoon ground cloves
- 1/4 teaspoon ground cardamom
- 1/4 teaspoon salt
- 1 cup unsalted butter, softened
- 1 1/2 cups granulated sugar
- 4 large eggs
- 1 teaspoon vanilla extract
- 1 cup brewed chai tea, cooled
- 1 cup sour cream

For the Spiced Buttercream:

- 1 cup unsalted butter, softened
- 4 cups powdered sugar
- 1/4 cup heavy cream
- 2 tablespoons brewed chai tea, cooled
- 1/2 teaspoon ground cinnamon
- Pinch of salt

Instructions:

1. **For the Chai Cake:**
    - Preheat your oven to 350°F (175°C). Grease and flour three 8-inch cake pans.
    - In a medium bowl, whisk together the flour, baking powder, baking soda, spices, and salt.
    - In a large bowl, beat the butter and sugar until light and fluffy. Add the eggs one at a time, mixing well after each addition. Stir in the vanilla extract.

- Gradually add the dry ingredients to the wet ingredients, alternating with the brewed chai tea and sour cream. Mix until smooth.
- Divide the batter evenly between the cake pans and bake for 25-30 minutes, or until a toothpick comes out clean. Cool the cakes in the pans for 10 minutes, then transfer to a wire rack to cool completely.

2. **For the Spiced Buttercream:**
    - Beat the butter until smooth and creamy.
    - Gradually add the powdered sugar, one cup at a time, and continue beating until fluffy.
    - Add the heavy cream, chai tea, cinnamon, and salt. Mix until smooth.

3. **Assembling the Cake:**
    - Place one layer of chai cake on a serving plate and spread with spiced buttercream.
    - Repeat with the second layer of cake and frosting.
    - Frost the entire cake with the remaining buttercream.

White Chocolate and Lemon Wedding Cake

Ingredients:

For the White Chocolate Cake:

- 2 1/2 cups all-purpose flour
- 2 teaspoons baking powder
- 1/2 teaspoon salt
- 1 cup unsalted butter, softened
- 1 1/2 cups granulated sugar
- 4 large eggs
- 1 teaspoon vanilla extract
- 1/2 cup white chocolate, melted
- 1 cup whole milk
- Zest of 1 lemon

For the Lemon Filling:

- 1 cup fresh lemon juice
- 1/2 cup granulated sugar
- 2 tablespoons cornstarch
- 1/2 teaspoon lemon zest

For the White Chocolate Buttercream:

- 1 cup unsalted butter, softened
- 4 cups powdered sugar
- 1/4 cup heavy cream
- 1/2 cup white chocolate, melted
- 1 teaspoon vanilla extract

Instructions:

1. **For the White Chocolate Cake:**
    - Preheat the oven to 350°F (175°C). Grease and flour three 8-inch cake pans.
    - In a medium bowl, whisk together the flour, baking powder, and salt.
    - In a large bowl, beat the butter and sugar until fluffy. Add the eggs one at a time, beating well after each addition. Stir in the vanilla extract.
    - Gradually add the dry ingredients, alternating with the milk, and mix until smooth.

- Stir in the melted white chocolate and lemon zest.
- Divide the batter evenly between the cake pans and bake for 25-30 minutes, or until a toothpick inserted comes out clean. Cool the cakes in the pans for 10 minutes, then transfer to a wire rack to cool completely.

2. **For the Lemon Filling:**
    - In a saucepan, whisk together lemon juice, sugar, and cornstarch. Cook over medium heat, stirring constantly, until thickened.
    - Stir in the lemon zest and remove from heat. Allow it to cool.
3. **For the White Chocolate Buttercream:**
    - Beat the butter until smooth.
    - Gradually add powdered sugar, one cup at a time, beating until fluffy.
    - Add the heavy cream, melted white chocolate, and vanilla extract. Beat until smooth.
4. **Assembling the Cake:**
    - Place one layer of cake on a serving plate and spread with lemon filling.
    - Top with a layer of white chocolate buttercream and repeat with the next layer.
    - Frost the entire cake with the remaining buttercream.

Strawberry Shortcake Wedding Cake

Ingredients:

For the Cake:

- 2 1/2 cups all-purpose flour
- 1 tablespoon baking powder
- 1/2 teaspoon salt
- 1 cup unsalted butter, softened
- 1 1/2 cups granulated sugar
- 4 large eggs
- 1 teaspoon vanilla extract
- 1 cup heavy cream

For the Strawberry Filling:

- 3 cups fresh strawberries, sliced
- 1/4 cup granulated sugar
- 1 tablespoon lemon juice

For the Whipped Cream:

- 2 cups heavy cream
- 1/4 cup powdered sugar
- 1 teaspoon vanilla extract

Instructions:

1. **For the Cake:**
    - Preheat your oven to 350°F (175°C). Grease and flour three 8-inch cake pans.
    - In a medium bowl, whisk together the flour, baking powder, and salt.
    - In a large bowl, beat the butter and sugar until light and fluffy. Add the eggs one at a time, mixing well after each addition. Stir in the vanilla extract.
    - Gradually add the dry ingredients, alternating with the heavy cream, until smooth.
    - Divide the batter evenly between the pans and bake for 25-30 minutes. Let the cakes cool.
2. **For the Strawberry Filling:**

    - Toss the sliced strawberries with sugar and lemon juice. Let them sit for 30 minutes to release their juices.
3. **For the Whipped Cream:**
    - Beat the heavy cream, powdered sugar, and vanilla until stiff peaks form.
4. **Assembling the Cake:**
    - Place one layer of cake, top with whipped cream and strawberries. Repeat for the second layer.
    - Finish with the final layer and a generous topping of whipped cream and strawberries.

Lemon and Rosemary Wedding Cake

Ingredients:

For the Lemon Cake:

- 2 1/2 cups all-purpose flour
- 2 teaspoons baking powder
- 1/2 teaspoon salt
- 1 cup unsalted butter, softened
- 1 1/2 cups granulated sugar
- 4 large eggs
- 1 teaspoon vanilla extract
- 2 teaspoons lemon zest
- 1/2 cup fresh lemon juice
- 1 cup buttermilk

For the Rosemary Buttercream:

- 1 cup unsalted butter, softened
- 4 cups powdered sugar
- 1/4 cup heavy cream
- 1 teaspoon lemon extract
- 1 tablespoon fresh rosemary, finely chopped

Instructions:

1. **For the Lemon Cake:**
    - Preheat your oven to 350°F (175°C). Grease and flour three 8-inch round cake pans.
    - In a medium bowl, whisk together the flour, baking powder, and salt.
    - In a large bowl, beat the butter and sugar until fluffy. Add the eggs one at a time, mixing well after each addition. Stir in the vanilla extract, lemon zest, and lemon juice.
    - Gradually add the dry ingredients, alternating with the buttermilk.
    - Divide the batter evenly between the pans and bake for 25-30 minutes. Cool completely.
2. **For the Rosemary Buttercream:**
    - Beat the butter until smooth and creamy.
    - Gradually add the powdered sugar and beat until fluffy.

- Add the heavy cream, lemon extract, and chopped rosemary. Mix until smooth.
3. **Assembling the Cake:**
    - Place one layer of cake on a serving plate, frost with rosemary buttercream, and repeat with the second and third layers.
    - Frost the entire cake with the rosemary buttercream.

Honey and Pear Wedding Cake

Ingredients:

For the Pear Cake:

- 2 1/2 cups all-purpose flour
- 1 teaspoon baking powder
- 1/2 teaspoon baking soda
- 1/2 teaspoon salt
- 1 cup unsalted butter, softened
- 1 1/2 cups granulated sugar
- 4 large eggs
- 1 teaspoon vanilla extract
- 1 cup pureed ripe pears
- 1/4 cup honey
- 1/2 cup buttermilk

For the Honey Buttercream:

- 1 cup unsalted butter, softened
- 4 cups powdered sugar
- 1/4 cup heavy cream
- 1/4 cup honey
- 1 teaspoon vanilla extract

Instructions:

1. **For the Pear Cake:**
    - Preheat your oven to 350°F (175°C). Grease and flour three 8-inch round cake pans.
    - In a medium bowl, whisk together the flour, baking powder, baking soda, and salt.
    - In a large bowl, beat the butter and sugar until light and fluffy. Add the eggs one at a time, mixing well after each addition. Stir in the vanilla extract, pear puree, and honey.
    - Gradually add the dry ingredients, alternating with the buttermilk. Mix until smooth.
    - Divide the batter between the cake pans and bake for 25-30 minutes. Cool completely.
2. **For the Honey Buttercream:**

- Beat the butter until creamy.
- Gradually add the powdered sugar, then mix in the heavy cream, honey, and vanilla extract. Beat until smooth and fluffy.
3. **Assembling the Cake:**
    - Place one layer of cake on a serving plate, frost with honey buttercream, and repeat with the remaining layers.
    - Frost the entire cake with the remaining buttercream.

Gingerbread Spice Wedding Cake:

Ingredients:

For the Gingerbread Spice Cake:

- 2 ½ cups all-purpose flour
- 1 ½ tsp baking powder
- 1 tsp baking soda
- 2 tsp ground ginger
- 1 ½ tsp ground cinnamon
- ½ tsp ground nutmeg
- ¼ tsp ground cloves
- ½ tsp salt
- ¾ cup unsalted butter, softened
- 1 cup brown sugar, packed
- 3 large eggs
- 1 cup molasses
- 1 cup buttermilk
- 1 tsp vanilla extract

For the Spiced Cream Cheese Frosting:

- 8 oz cream cheese, softened
- ½ cup unsalted butter, softened
- 4 cups powdered sugar
- 1 tsp ground cinnamon
- 1/2 tsp ground ginger
- ½ tsp vanilla extract
- Pinch of salt

Instructions:

1. Prepare the Cake:

- Preheat your oven to 350°F (175°C). Grease and flour three 9-inch round cake pans.
- In a medium bowl, whisk together the flour, baking powder, baking soda, spices, and salt. Set aside.
- In a large bowl, cream the butter and brown sugar together until light and fluffy, about 3-4 minutes.

- Add the eggs one at a time, mixing well after each addition. Stir in the molasses and vanilla extract.
- Gradually add the dry ingredients to the wet mixture, alternating with the buttermilk. Start and end with the dry ingredients, mixing until just combined.
- Divide the batter evenly among the prepared cake pans. Smooth the tops.
- Bake for 25-30 minutes, or until a toothpick inserted into the center of the cakes comes out clean. Allow the cakes to cool in the pans for 10 minutes, then transfer to wire racks to cool completely.

2. Make the Spiced Cream Cheese Frosting:

- In a large bowl, beat together the softened cream cheese and butter until smooth and creamy.
- Gradually add the powdered sugar, a cup at a time, beating until smooth.
- Stir in the cinnamon, ginger, vanilla extract, and a pinch of salt. Beat until the frosting is light and fluffy.

3. Assemble the Cake:

- Once the cakes are completely cooled, place the first layer on a cake stand or serving platter.
- Spread a layer of frosting over the top of the first cake layer.
- Place the second layer on top and repeat the frosting layer. Repeat with the third layer.
- Frost the top and sides of the entire cake with the remaining frosting.
- Decorate the cake with additional spices or festive toppings, such as cinnamon sticks or candied ginger slices, if desired.

Blueberry and Vanilla Wedding Cake

Ingredients:

For the Blueberry Cake:

- 2 ½ cups all-purpose flour
- 2 tsp baking powder
- ½ tsp salt
- 1 cup unsalted butter, softened
- 1 ½ cups granulated sugar
- 4 large eggs
- 1 tbsp vanilla extract
- 1 cup whole milk
- 1 ½ cups fresh blueberries (or frozen, if needed)

For the Vanilla Buttercream:

- 1 cup unsalted butter, softened
- 4 cups powdered sugar
- 1 tbsp vanilla extract
- 2 tbsp whole milk
- Pinch of salt

Instructions:

1. **Make the Blueberry Cake:**
    - Preheat the oven to 350°F (175°C). Grease and flour three 9-inch round cake pans.
    - In a medium bowl, whisk together the flour, baking powder, and salt. Set aside.
    - In a large bowl, cream the butter and sugar together until light and fluffy.
    - Add the eggs one at a time, mixing well after each addition. Stir in the vanilla extract.
    - Gradually add the dry ingredients in three parts, alternating with the milk. Mix until smooth.
    - Gently fold in the blueberries.
    - Divide the batter between the cake pans. Bake for 25-30 minutes, or until a toothpick inserted into the center comes out clean. Allow to cool in the pans for 10 minutes, then transfer to wire racks to cool completely.
2. **Make the Vanilla Buttercream:**

- In a large bowl, beat the butter until smooth and creamy.
        - Gradually add the powdered sugar, beating until light and fluffy.
        - Mix in the vanilla extract, milk, and salt.
3. **Assemble the Cake:**
     - Once the cakes are completely cooled, frost each layer with the vanilla buttercream. Stack the layers and frost the top and sides of the entire cake. Garnish with fresh blueberries or edible flowers, if desired.

Pomegranate and White Chocolate Wedding Cake

Ingredients:

For the Pomegranate Cake:

- 2 ½ cups all-purpose flour
- 2 tsp baking powder
- ½ tsp salt
- 1 cup unsalted butter, softened
- 1 ½ cups granulated sugar
- 4 large eggs
- 1 tsp vanilla extract
- 1 cup pomegranate juice
- 1 cup buttermilk
- 1 cup pomegranate seeds (for garnish)

For the White Chocolate Buttercream:

- 8 oz white chocolate, melted
- 1 cup unsalted butter, softened
- 4 cups powdered sugar
- 2 tbsp heavy cream
- 1 tsp vanilla extract

Instructions:

1. **Make the Pomegranate Cake:**
    - Preheat the oven to 350°F (175°C). Grease and flour three 9-inch round cake pans.
    - In a medium bowl, whisk together the flour, baking powder, and salt. Set aside.
    - In a large bowl, cream the butter and sugar together until light and fluffy.
    - Add the eggs one at a time, mixing well after each addition. Stir in the vanilla extract.
    - Gradually add the dry ingredients, alternating with the pomegranate juice and buttermilk. Mix until smooth.
    - Divide the batter between the cake pans. Bake for 25-30 minutes, or until a toothpick inserted comes out clean. Allow to cool completely.
2. **Make the White Chocolate Buttercream:**

- Melt the white chocolate in a heatproof bowl over a double boiler or in the microwave. Allow to cool slightly.
- In a large bowl, beat the butter until smooth and creamy.
- Gradually add the powdered sugar and beat until fluffy.
- Stir in the melted white chocolate, heavy cream, and vanilla extract.

3. **Assemble the Cake:**
   - Frost each layer of the cooled cake with the white chocolate buttercream.
   - Once all layers are stacked, frost the top and sides of the cake with the remaining buttercream.
   - Garnish with pomegranate seeds on top for a touch of color and elegance.

Mint Chocolate Chip Wedding Cake

Ingredients:

For the Mint Chocolate Cake:

- 2 ½ cups all-purpose flour
- 1 ½ tsp baking powder
- ½ tsp salt
- ¾ cup unsweetened cocoa powder
- 1 cup unsalted butter, softened
- 1 ½ cups granulated sugar
- 4 large eggs
- 1 tsp mint extract
- 1 cup whole milk
- 1 ½ cups mini chocolate chips

For the Mint Buttercream:

- 1 cup unsalted butter, softened
- 4 cups powdered sugar
- 1 tbsp mint extract
- 3-4 tbsp heavy cream
- Green food coloring (optional)
- 1 cup mini chocolate chips (for garnish)

Instructions:

1. **Make the Mint Chocolate Cake:**
   - Preheat the oven to 350°F (175°C). Grease and flour three 9-inch round cake pans.
   - In a medium bowl, whisk together the flour, baking powder, salt, and cocoa powder. Set aside.
   - In a large bowl, cream the butter and sugar together until light and fluffy.
   - Add the eggs one at a time, mixing well after each addition. Stir in the mint extract.
   - Gradually add the dry ingredients, alternating with the milk, mixing until just combined.
   - Fold in the mini chocolate chips.
   - Divide the batter between the cake pans. Bake for 25-30 minutes, or until a toothpick comes out clean. Allow to cool completely.

2. **Make the Mint Buttercream:**
    - In a large bowl, beat the butter until smooth and creamy.
    - Gradually add the powdered sugar, beating until light and fluffy.
    - Stir in the mint extract and heavy cream. Add a few drops of green food coloring if desired.
3. **Assemble the Cake:**
    - Frost each layer of cake with the mint buttercream.
    - Once stacked, frost the top and sides with the remaining buttercream.
    - Garnish with mini chocolate chips on top for extra decoration and texture.

Mango and Coconut Wedding Cake

Ingredients:

For the Mango Cake:

- 2 ½ cups all-purpose flour
- 2 tsp baking powder
- ½ tsp salt
- 1 cup unsalted butter, softened
- 1 ½ cups granulated sugar
- 4 large eggs
- 1 cup mango puree (fresh or canned)
- 1 tsp vanilla extract
- ½ cup shredded coconut (unsweetened)
- ½ cup coconut milk

For the Coconut Buttercream:

- 1 cup unsalted butter, softened
- 4 cups powdered sugar
- 1 tsp vanilla extract
- 2 tbsp coconut milk
- 1 cup shredded coconut (for garnish)

Instructions:

1. **Make the Mango Cake:**
    - Preheat the oven to 350°F (175°C). Grease and flour three 9-inch round cake pans.
    - In a medium bowl, whisk together the flour, baking powder, and salt. Set aside.
    - In a large bowl, cream the butter and sugar together until light and fluffy.
    - Add the eggs one at a time, mixing well after each addition. Stir in the mango puree and vanilla extract.
    - Gradually add the dry ingredients, alternating with coconut milk, and mix until smooth.
    - Gently fold in the shredded coconut.
    - Divide the batter evenly between the cake pans. Bake for 25-30 minutes, or until a toothpick comes out clean. Let the cakes cool in the pans for 10 minutes, then transfer to wire racks to cool completely.

2. **Make the Coconut Buttercream:**
    - In a large bowl, beat the butter until creamy.
    - Gradually add the powdered sugar and beat until fluffy.
    - Stir in the vanilla extract and coconut milk until smooth and well combined.
3. **Assemble the Cake:**
    - Frost each layer of the cooled mango cake with the coconut buttercream.
    - Stack the layers and frost the top and sides of the entire cake.
    - Garnish with shredded coconut on top and around the edges for decoration.

Champagne and Peach Wedding Cake

Ingredients:

For the Champagne Cake:

- 2 ½ cups all-purpose flour
- 2 tsp baking powder
- ½ tsp salt
- 1 cup unsalted butter, softened
- 1 ½ cups granulated sugar
- 4 large eggs
- 1 tsp vanilla extract
- 1 cup champagne (or sparkling wine)
- ½ cup sour cream

For the Peach Buttercream:

- 1 cup unsalted butter, softened
- 4 cups powdered sugar
- 1 tsp vanilla extract
- 2 tbsp peach puree (fresh or canned)
- 2 tbsp champagne or sparkling wine
- A few drops of peach extract (optional, for a more intense peach flavor)

Instructions:

1. **Make the Champagne Cake:**
   - Preheat the oven to 350°F (175°C). Grease and flour three 9-inch round cake pans.
   - In a medium bowl, whisk together the flour, baking powder, and salt. Set aside.
   - In a large bowl, cream the butter and sugar together until light and fluffy.
   - Add the eggs one at a time, mixing well after each addition. Stir in the vanilla extract.
   - Gradually add the dry ingredients, alternating with the champagne and sour cream, mixing until smooth.
   - Divide the batter evenly between the cake pans. Bake for 25-30 minutes, or until a toothpick comes out clean. Cool completely.
2. **Make the Peach Buttercream:**
   - In a large bowl, beat the butter until smooth and creamy.

- Gradually add the powdered sugar, beating until fluffy.
- Stir in the peach puree, champagne, and vanilla extract until well combined.
- If you'd like a more intense peach flavor, add a few drops of peach extract.

3. **Assemble the Cake:**
   - Frost each layer of the cooled champagne cake with the peach buttercream.
   - Once all layers are stacked, frost the top and sides of the cake with the remaining buttercream.

Coconut Cream Wedding Cake

Ingredients:

For the Coconut Cake:

- 2 ½ cups all-purpose flour
- 2 tsp baking powder
- ½ tsp salt
- 1 cup unsalted butter, softened
- 1 ½ cups granulated sugar
- 4 large eggs
- 1 cup canned coconut milk
- 1 tsp vanilla extract
- 1 ½ cups shredded coconut (unsweetened)

For the Coconut Cream Filling:

- 1 cup heavy cream
- 1 cup coconut cream
- ¼ cup powdered sugar
- ½ tsp vanilla extract

For the Coconut Buttercream:

- 1 cup unsalted butter, softened
- 4 cups powdered sugar
- 1 tsp vanilla extract
- 3-4 tbsp coconut milk
- 1 ½ cups shredded coconut (for garnish)

Instructions:

1. **Make the Coconut Cake:**
    - Preheat the oven to 350°F (175°C). Grease and flour three 9-inch round cake pans.
    - In a medium bowl, whisk together the flour, baking powder, and salt. Set aside.
    - In a large bowl, cream the butter and sugar together until light and fluffy.
    - Add the eggs one at a time, mixing well after each addition. Stir in the coconut milk and vanilla extract.
    - Gradually add the dry ingredients and mix until smooth.

- Fold in the shredded coconut.
 - Divide the batter evenly between the cake pans. Bake for 25-30 minutes, or until a toothpick comes out clean. Let the cakes cool in the pans for 10 minutes, then transfer to wire racks to cool completely.
2. **Make the Coconut Cream Filling:**
   - In a chilled mixing bowl, whip the heavy cream, coconut cream, powdered sugar, and vanilla extract together until stiff peaks form.
3. **Make the Coconut Buttercream:**
   - In a large bowl, beat the butter until smooth and creamy.
   - Gradually add the powdered sugar, beating until fluffy.
   - Stir in the vanilla extract and coconut milk, adjusting the milk to reach your desired consistency.
4. **Assemble the Cake:**
   - Frost each layer of the cooled coconut cake with coconut buttercream.
   - After stacking the layers, pipe or spread coconut cream filling in the middle of each layer.
   - Frost the top and sides with the remaining buttercream.
   - Garnish with shredded coconut on top and around the sides.

Black Forest Wedding Cake

Ingredients:

For the Chocolate Cake:

- 2 ½ cups all-purpose flour
- 2 ½ tsp baking powder
- 1 ½ tsp baking soda
- ¾ cup unsweetened cocoa powder
- 1 ½ cups granulated sugar
- 1 tsp salt
- 2 large eggs
- 1 cup whole milk
- 1/2 cup vegetable oil
- 1 tsp vanilla extract
- 1 cup boiling water

For the Cherry Filling:

- 2 cups fresh or frozen cherries (pitted)
- ½ cup granulated sugar
- 1 tbsp cornstarch
- 1 tbsp water
- 2 tbsp Kirsch (cherry liqueur) (optional)

For the Whipped Cream:

- 2 cups heavy whipping cream
- ¼ cup powdered sugar
- 1 tsp vanilla extract

Instructions:

1. **Make the Chocolate Cake:**
    - Preheat the oven to 350°F (175°C). Grease and flour three 9-inch round cake pans.
    - In a large bowl, sift together the flour, baking powder, baking soda, cocoa powder, sugar, and salt.
    - Add the eggs, milk, vegetable oil, and vanilla extract to the dry ingredients. Beat until smooth.

- Gradually add the boiling water and mix until well combined. The batter will be thin.
- Divide the batter evenly between the prepared pans and bake for 30-35 minutes, or until a toothpick comes out clean. Let the cakes cool in the pans for 10 minutes before transferring to wire racks to cool completely.

2. **Make the Cherry Filling:**
    - In a medium saucepan, combine the cherries, sugar, cornstarch, and water. Cook over medium heat, stirring constantly until the mixture thickens and the cherries release their juices, about 5-7 minutes.
    - Remove from heat and stir in the Kirsch, if using. Let the cherry filling cool to room temperature.
3. **Make the Whipped Cream:**
    - In a large bowl, beat the heavy cream, powdered sugar, and vanilla extract until stiff peaks form.
4. **Assemble the Cake:**
    - Once the cakes are completely cooled, slice each cake in half horizontally.
    - Place one layer of cake on a serving platter and spread a layer of cherry filling over it.
    - Add a layer of whipped cream and top with another layer of cake. Repeat the process with the remaining layers.
    - Frost the top and sides of the cake with whipped cream, and garnish with additional cherries and shaved chocolate.

Raspberry and Vanilla Wedding Cake

Ingredients:

For the Vanilla Cake:

- 2 ½ cups all-purpose flour
- 2 tsp baking powder
- ½ tsp salt
- 1 cup unsalted butter, softened
- 2 cups granulated sugar
- 4 large eggs
- 2 tsp vanilla extract
- 1 cup whole milk

For the Raspberry Filling:

- 2 cups fresh raspberries (or frozen, thawed)
- ¾ cup granulated sugar
- 1 tbsp lemon juice
- 1 tbsp cornstarch
- ¼ cup water

For the Vanilla Buttercream:

- 1 cup unsalted butter, softened
- 4 cups powdered sugar
- 2 tsp vanilla extract
- 2-3 tbsp heavy cream or milk

Instructions:

1. **Make the Vanilla Cake:**
    - Preheat the oven to 350°F (175°C). Grease and flour three 9-inch round cake pans.
    - In a medium bowl, whisk together the flour, baking powder, and salt. Set aside.
    - In a large bowl, cream the butter and sugar until light and fluffy.
    - Add the eggs one at a time, mixing well after each addition. Stir in the vanilla extract.
    - Gradually add the dry ingredients, alternating with the milk, and mix until smooth.

- Divide the batter evenly between the prepared pans and bake for 25-30 minutes, or until a toothpick comes out clean. Let the cakes cool in the pans for 10 minutes before transferring to wire racks to cool completely.

2. **Make the Raspberry Filling:**
    - In a medium saucepan, combine the raspberries, sugar, lemon juice, cornstarch, and water. Cook over medium heat, stirring constantly until the mixture thickens and the raspberries break down, about 5-7 minutes.
    - Remove from heat and allow the raspberry filling to cool.
3. **Make the Vanilla Buttercream:**
    - In a large bowl, beat the butter until creamy.
    - Gradually add the powdered sugar, beating until smooth and fluffy.
    - Stir in the vanilla extract and enough heavy cream or milk to reach your desired consistency.
4. **Assemble the Cake:**
    - Once the cakes are completely cooled, slice each layer in half horizontally.
    - Place one layer of cake on a serving platter and spread a layer of raspberry filling over it.
    - Top with a layer of vanilla buttercream and another layer of cake. Repeat the process with the remaining layers.
    - Frost the top and sides of the cake with vanilla buttercream, and garnish with fresh raspberries on top.

Poppy Seed Lemon Wedding Cake

Ingredients:

For the Lemon Poppy Seed Cake:

- 2 ½ cups all-purpose flour
- 1 tbsp poppy seeds
- 2 tsp baking powder
- ½ tsp salt
- 1 cup unsalted butter, softened
- 2 cups granulated sugar
- 4 large eggs
- 2 tbsp lemon zest
- 1 ½ cups whole milk
- 2 tbsp lemon juice
- 1 tsp vanilla extract

For the Lemon Buttercream:

- 1 cup unsalted butter, softened
- 4 cups powdered sugar
- 2 tbsp lemon juice
- 2 tsp lemon zest
- 2-3 tbsp heavy cream or milk

Instructions:

1. **Make the Lemon Poppy Seed Cake:**
    - Preheat the oven to 350°F (175°C). Grease and flour three 9-inch round cake pans.
    - In a medium bowl, whisk together the flour, poppy seeds, baking powder, and salt. Set aside.
    - In a large bowl, cream the butter and sugar together until light and fluffy.
    - Add the eggs one at a time, mixing well after each addition. Stir in the lemon zest, lemon juice, and vanilla extract.
    - Gradually add the dry ingredients, alternating with the milk, mixing until smooth.
    - Divide the batter evenly between the prepared pans and bake for 25-30 minutes, or until a toothpick comes out clean. Let the cakes cool in the pans for 10 minutes before transferring to wire racks to cool completely.

2. **Make the Lemon Buttercream:**
    - In a large bowl, beat the butter until creamy.
    - Gradually add the powdered sugar, beating until smooth and fluffy.
    - Stir in the lemon juice and lemon zest, adding enough heavy cream or milk to reach the desired consistency.
3. **Assemble the Cake:**
    - Once the cakes are completely cooled, slice each layer in half horizontally.
    - Place one layer of cake on a serving platter and spread a layer of lemon buttercream over it.
    - Top with another layer of cake and repeat the process with the remaining layers.
    - Frost the top and sides of the cake with lemon buttercream and garnish with lemon zest or edible flowers for decoration.

Apricot Almond Wedding Cake

Ingredients:

For the Almond Cake:

- 2 ½ cups all-purpose flour
- 1 tsp baking powder
- ½ tsp salt
- 1 cup unsalted butter, softened
- 1 ½ cups granulated sugar
- 4 large eggs
- 1 ½ tsp almond extract
- 1 ½ cups whole milk
- 1 cup ground almonds (almond meal)

For the Apricot Filling:

- 2 cups apricot preserves or jam
- 1 tbsp lemon juice
- 1 tbsp water

For the Almond Buttercream:

- 1 cup unsalted butter, softened
- 4 cups powdered sugar
- 2 tsp almond extract
- 2-3 tbsp heavy cream or milk

Instructions:

1. **Make the Almond Cake:**
    - Preheat the oven to 350°F (175°C). Grease and flour three 9-inch round cake pans.
    - In a medium bowl, whisk together the flour, baking powder, and salt. Set aside.
    - In a large bowl, cream the butter and sugar together until light and fluffy.
    - Add the eggs one at a time, mixing well after each addition. Stir in the almond extract.
    - Gradually add the dry ingredients, alternating with the milk, and mix until smooth. Fold in the ground almonds.

- Divide the batter evenly between the prepared pans and bake for 25-30 minutes, or until a toothpick comes out clean. Let the cakes cool in the pans for 10 minutes before transferring to wire racks to cool completely.
2. **Make the Apricot Filling:**
    - In a small saucepan, combine the apricot preserves, lemon juice, and water. Heat over low heat, stirring until the preserves have melted and the mixture is smooth. Let it cool to room temperature.
3. **Make the Almond Buttercream:**
    - In a large bowl, beat the butter until creamy.
    - Gradually add the powdered sugar, beating until smooth and fluffy.
    - Stir in the almond extract and enough heavy cream or milk to reach the desired consistency.
4. **Assemble the Cake:**
    - Once the cakes are completely cooled, slice each layer in half horizontally.
    - Place one layer of cake on a serving platter and spread a layer of apricot filling over it.
    - Top with a layer of almond buttercream and another layer of cake. Repeat the process with the remaining layers.
    - Frost the top and sides of the cake with almond buttercream and garnish with toasted sliced almonds.

Tropical Fruit Wedding Cake

Ingredients:

For the Tropical Fruit Cake:

- 2 ½ cups all-purpose flour
- 2 tsp baking powder
- ½ tsp salt
- 1 cup unsalted butter, softened
- 2 cups granulated sugar
- 4 large eggs
- 1 tsp vanilla extract
- 1 cup unsweetened coconut milk
- 1 cup diced pineapple (fresh or canned)
- 1 cup diced mango
- ½ cup shredded coconut

For the Tropical Fruit Filling:

- 1 cup diced pineapple
- 1 cup diced mango
- ½ cup passion fruit pulp
- 1 tbsp sugar
- 1 tbsp lemon juice

For the Coconut Buttercream:

- 1 cup unsalted butter, softened
- 4 cups powdered sugar
- 2 tsp coconut extract
- 2-3 tbsp heavy cream or milk

Instructions:

1. **Make the Tropical Fruit Cake:**
   - Preheat the oven to 350°F (175°C). Grease and flour three 9-inch round cake pans.
   - In a medium bowl, whisk together the flour, baking powder, and salt. Set aside.
   - In a large bowl, cream the butter and sugar together until light and fluffy.

- Add the eggs one at a time, mixing well after each addition. Stir in the vanilla extract.
- Gradually add the dry ingredients, alternating with the coconut milk, mixing until smooth. Fold in the diced pineapple, mango, and shredded coconut.
- Divide the batter evenly between the prepared pans and bake for 30-35 minutes, or until a toothpick comes out clean. Let the cakes cool in the pans for 10 minutes before transferring to wire racks to cool completely.

2. **Make the Tropical Fruit Filling:**
    - In a small saucepan, combine the pineapple, mango, passion fruit pulp, sugar, and lemon juice. Heat over medium heat, stirring occasionally, until the mixture thickens, about 5-7 minutes. Let it cool.

3. **Make the Coconut Buttercream:**
    - In a large bowl, beat the butter until creamy.
    - Gradually add the powdered sugar, beating until smooth and fluffy.
    - Stir in the coconut extract and enough heavy cream or milk to reach the desired consistency.

4. **Assemble the Cake:**
    - Once the cakes are completely cooled, slice each layer in half horizontally.
    - Place one layer of cake on a serving platter and spread a layer of tropical fruit filling over it.
    - Top with a layer of coconut buttercream and another layer of cake. Repeat the process with the remaining layers.
    - Frost the top and sides of the cake with coconut buttercream and garnish with additional tropical fruit and toasted coconut flakes.

Chocolate and Bourbon Wedding Cake

Ingredients:

For the Chocolate Cake:

- 2 ½ cups all-purpose flour
- 2 tsp baking powder
- 1 ½ tsp baking soda
- ¾ cup unsweetened cocoa powder
- 1 ½ cups granulated sugar
- 1 tsp salt
- 2 large eggs
- 1 cup buttermilk
- ½ cup vegetable oil
- 1 tsp vanilla extract
- 1 cup hot brewed coffee
- ¼ cup bourbon

For the Bourbon Chocolate Ganache:

- 8 oz semisweet chocolate, chopped
- ½ cup heavy cream
- 2 tbsp bourbon
- 1 tbsp unsalted butter

For the Bourbon Buttercream:

- 1 cup unsalted butter, softened
- 4 cups powdered sugar
- 2 tbsp bourbon
- 2 tbsp heavy cream
- 1 tsp vanilla extract

Instructions:

1. **Make the Chocolate Cake:**
    - Preheat the oven to 350°F (175°C). Grease and flour three 9-inch round cake pans.
    - In a large bowl, sift together the flour, baking powder, baking soda, cocoa powder, sugar, and salt.

- In a separate bowl, whisk together the eggs, buttermilk, vegetable oil, and vanilla extract.
- Gradually add the wet ingredients to the dry ingredients and mix until smooth.
- Stir in the hot coffee and bourbon. The batter will be thin.
- Divide the batter evenly between the prepared pans and bake for 30-35 minutes, or until a toothpick comes out clean. Let the cakes cool in the pans for 10 minutes before transferring to wire racks to cool completely.

2. **Make the Bourbon Chocolate Ganache:**
   - In a small saucepan, heat the heavy cream over medium heat until it begins to simmer.
   - Pour the hot cream over the chopped chocolate and let it sit for 1-2 minutes, then stir until smooth.
   - Stir in the bourbon and butter, mixing until glossy. Let the ganache cool to room temperature.

3. **Make the Bourbon Buttercream:**
   - In a large bowl, beat the butter until creamy.
   - Gradually add the powdered sugar, beating until smooth and fluffy.
   - Stir in the bourbon, heavy cream, and vanilla extract, mixing until smooth and fluffy.

4. **Assemble the Cake:**
   - Once the cakes are completely cooled, slice each layer in half horizontally.
   - Place one layer of cake on a serving platter and spread a layer of bourbon chocolate ganache over it.
   - Top with a layer of bourbon buttercream and another layer of cake. Repeat the process with the remaining layers.
   - Frost the top and sides of the cake with bourbon buttercream, and drizzle with more bourbon chocolate ganache. Decorate with chocolate shavings or cocoa powder.

Wildflower Honey Wedding Cake

Ingredients for the cake:

- 3 cups all-purpose flour
- 2 tsp baking powder
- 1/2 tsp baking soda
- 1/2 tsp salt
- 1 cup unsalted butter, softened
- 1 1/2 cups wildflower honey
- 4 large eggs
- 1 tsp vanilla extract
- 1 cup whole milk
- 1/2 cup sour cream
- 1 tbsp lemon zest (optional)

Ingredients for the frosting:

- 2 cups heavy cream
- 8 oz mascarpone cheese, softened
- 1/2 cup powdered sugar
- 1 tsp vanilla extract
- 1 tbsp wildflower honey (optional for extra sweetness)

Instructions:

1. Preheat oven to 350°F (175°C). Grease and flour three 9-inch round cake pans.
2. In a bowl, whisk together flour, baking powder, baking soda, and salt.
3. In a separate bowl, beat butter and honey until light and fluffy. Add eggs one at a time, mixing well after each addition. Stir in vanilla extract.
4. Gradually add dry ingredients, alternating with milk and sour cream, until smooth.
5. Pour batter evenly into the prepared pans and bake for 25-30 minutes or until a toothpick inserted comes out clean.
6. While the cakes cool, beat the heavy cream until stiff peaks form. In a separate bowl, whisk mascarpone, powdered sugar, vanilla extract, and honey.
7. Gently fold whipped cream into the mascarpone mixture.
8. Frost the cooled cakes with mascarpone frosting, and if desired, drizzle with additional wildflower honey.

Red Wine and Chocolate Wedding Cake

Ingredients for the cake:

- 2 cups all-purpose flour
- 1 1/2 cups granulated sugar
- 1 tsp baking powder
- 1 tsp baking soda
- 1/2 tsp salt
- 3/4 cup unsweetened cocoa powder
- 1 cup red wine (preferably a dry red wine like Cabernet Sauvignon)
- 1/2 cup buttermilk
- 2 large eggs
- 1 tsp vanilla extract
- 1/2 cup unsalted butter, softened

Ingredients for the frosting:

- 8 oz dark chocolate, chopped
- 1 cup heavy cream
- 1/2 cup unsalted butter, softened
- 2 cups powdered sugar
- 1 tsp vanilla extract

Instructions:

1. Preheat oven to 350°F (175°C). Grease and flour two 9-inch round cake pans.
2. In a bowl, whisk together flour, sugar, baking powder, baking soda, salt, and cocoa powder.
3. In a separate bowl, beat butter and eggs until smooth. Add wine, buttermilk, and vanilla extract, mixing until combined.
4. Gradually add dry ingredients and mix until smooth.
5. Pour batter into the pans and bake for 30-35 minutes, or until a toothpick inserted comes out clean.
6. While the cake cools, prepare the frosting. Melt dark chocolate and heavy cream together in a double boiler or microwave. Stir until smooth and allow to cool slightly.
7. Beat the softened butter with powdered sugar until smooth. Gradually add the cooled chocolate mixture, beating until combined.

8. Frost the cooled cakes with the rich chocolate frosting, smoothing the top and sides.

Marzipan and Dark Chocolate Wedding Cake

Ingredients for the cake:

- 2 1/2 cups all-purpose flour
- 1 1/2 cups granulated sugar
- 1 tsp baking powder
- 1/2 tsp baking soda
- 1/2 tsp salt
- 1 1/2 cups unsalted butter, softened
- 3/4 cup marzipan, grated or finely chopped
- 4 large eggs
- 1 tsp vanilla extract
- 1/2 cup whole milk
- 1/2 cup almond milk

Ingredients for the frosting:

- 8 oz dark chocolate, chopped
- 1/2 cup unsalted butter, softened
- 2 cups powdered sugar
- 1 tsp vanilla extract
- 1/4 cup heavy cream
- 1/2 cup marzipan, finely chopped (for garnish)

Instructions:

1. Preheat oven to 350°F (175°C). Grease and flour two 9-inch round cake pans.
2. In a bowl, whisk together flour, baking powder, baking soda, and salt.
3. In a separate bowl, beat butter and sugar until creamy. Add eggs one at a time, mixing well after each addition. Stir in vanilla extract and grated marzipan.
4. Gradually add dry ingredients, alternating with whole milk and almond milk, until smooth.
5. Pour batter into the pans and bake for 25-30 minutes, or until a toothpick comes out clean.
6. For the frosting, melt dark chocolate and butter together in a double boiler or microwave. Stir until smooth.
7. Allow the chocolate mixture to cool slightly, then beat in powdered sugar and vanilla extract.

8. Add heavy cream to adjust the frosting consistency. Frost the cooled cakes with the dark chocolate frosting.
9. Garnish with finely chopped marzipan on top for an elegant finish.

Apple Cinnamon Wedding Cake

Ingredients for the cake:

- 3 cups all-purpose flour
- 1 1/2 tsp baking powder
- 1 tsp baking soda
- 1 tsp ground cinnamon
- 1/2 tsp ground nutmeg
- 1/2 tsp salt
- 1 cup unsalted butter, softened
- 2 cups granulated sugar
- 4 large eggs
- 2 tsp vanilla extract
- 1 cup unsweetened applesauce
- 1/2 cup milk
- 2 cups diced apples (preferably Granny Smith)

Ingredients for the frosting:

- 8 oz cream cheese, softened
- 1/2 cup unsalted butter, softened
- 4 cups powdered sugar
- 1 tsp vanilla extract
- 1 tsp ground cinnamon
- 1-2 tbsp heavy cream (for desired consistency)

Instructions:

1. Preheat oven to 350°F (175°C). Grease and flour two 9-inch round cake pans.
2. In a bowl, whisk together flour, baking powder, baking soda, cinnamon, nutmeg, and salt.
3. In a separate large bowl, beat the butter and sugar together until light and fluffy. Add eggs one at a time, mixing well after each addition. Stir in vanilla extract.
4. Gradually add the dry ingredients to the wet ingredients, alternating with applesauce and milk, until smooth.
5. Gently fold in diced apples.
6. Divide the batter between the prepared pans and bake for 30-35 minutes, or until a toothpick inserted comes out clean.

7. While the cakes cool, prepare the frosting. Beat cream cheese and butter together until smooth. Gradually add powdered sugar, cinnamon, and vanilla extract. Beat until fluffy, adding heavy cream to adjust consistency.
8. Frost the cooled cakes with the cream cheese frosting, and garnish with cinnamon or apple slices if desired.

Almond and Cherry Wedding Cake

Ingredients for the cake:

- 2 1/2 cups all-purpose flour
- 1 1/2 tsp baking powder
- 1/2 tsp salt
- 1 cup unsalted butter, softened
- 1 1/2 cups granulated sugar
- 4 large eggs
- 1 tsp almond extract
- 1/2 tsp vanilla extract
- 1/2 cup whole milk
- 1/2 cup maraschino cherry juice
- 1 cup chopped maraschino cherries

Ingredients for the frosting:

- 8 oz cream cheese, softened
- 1 cup unsalted butter, softened
- 4 cups powdered sugar
- 1 tsp vanilla extract
- 1 tsp almond extract
- 1/2 cup chopped maraschino cherries (for garnish)

Instructions:

1. Preheat oven to 350°F (175°C). Grease and flour two 9-inch round cake pans.
2. In a bowl, whisk together flour, baking powder, and salt.
3. In a separate large bowl, beat the butter and sugar until light and fluffy. Add eggs one at a time, mixing well after each addition. Stir in almond and vanilla extracts.
4. Gradually add the dry ingredients to the wet ingredients, alternating with milk and cherry juice, until smooth.
5. Gently fold in chopped cherries.
6. Divide the batter between the prepared pans and bake for 30-35 minutes, or until a toothpick inserted comes out clean.
7. While the cakes cool, prepare the frosting. Beat cream cheese and butter until smooth. Gradually add powdered sugar, almond extract, and vanilla extract. Beat until fluffy.

8. Frost the cooled cakes with the frosting and garnish with chopped maraschino cherries for a festive touch.

Citrus and Coconut Wedding Cake

Ingredients for the cake:

- 3 cups all-purpose flour
- 1 1/2 tsp baking powder
- 1/2 tsp baking soda
- 1/2 tsp salt
- 1 cup unsalted butter, softened
- 2 cups granulated sugar
- 4 large eggs
- 1/2 cup fresh orange juice
- 1 tsp orange zest
- 1/2 cup unsweetened shredded coconut
- 1/2 cup whole milk

Ingredients for the frosting:

- 8 oz cream cheese, softened
- 1 cup unsalted butter, softened
- 4 cups powdered sugar
- 1 tsp vanilla extract
- 1/2 tsp orange extract
- 1/4 cup shredded coconut (for garnish)
- Orange slices or zest (for garnish)

Instructions:

1. Preheat oven to 350°F (175°C). Grease and flour two 9-inch round cake pans.
2. In a bowl, whisk together flour, baking powder, baking soda, and salt.
3. In a separate large bowl, beat the butter and sugar together until light and fluffy. Add eggs one at a time, mixing well after each addition. Stir in orange juice, orange zest, and shredded coconut.
4. Gradually add the dry ingredients to the wet ingredients, alternating with milk, until smooth.
5. Divide the batter between the prepared pans and bake for 30-35 minutes, or until a toothpick inserted comes out clean.
6. While the cakes cool, prepare the frosting. Beat cream cheese and butter until smooth. Gradually add powdered sugar, vanilla extract, and orange extract. Beat until fluffy.

7. Frost the cooled cakes with the citrus-infused frosting, and garnish with shredded coconut, orange slices, or zest for a fresh, tropical finish.